Islay & Jura

Lindsey Porter

ISLAY AND JURA

A complex geological structure has contributed to giving this Inner Hebridean island a captivating landscape moulded by time to create memorable vistas. It has an ancient heritage witnessed by the Kildalton Cross which has survived the ravages of Atlantic winters for nearly a millennium. Moreover, Islay (pronounced I- la) lies adjacent to the island of Jura, perhaps better known for its whisky, an island of significant size yet as different from Islay as can be imagined.

Jura shares one economic feature with Islay: whisky. It has a distillery situated on the coast, carefully and patiently producing a fine and popular series of malts. Islay has its distilleries too. In fact it has no less than eight of them, with another on the way, most of them on the coast and all with a name familiar to whisky drinkers (and some even possibly familiar names to many of those that aren't whisky drinkers).

Despite having a population of c. 3,500 (1901: 6,857), Islay has avoided adopting an urban feel to it. It retains its island identity just like Jura; that special characteristic that draws visitors but is difficult to define. However it isn't just whisky of course which brings the visitors or that ever-special island atmosphere; its lochs attract many breeds of waterfowl let alone the impressive list of species of birds in general. Jura is primarily a series of sporting estates for the deer, on land so poor it will support nothing better. It is nonetheless an important contributor to the island's economy. These estates also support an abundant and protected wildlife other than deer, let alone an undisturbed flora etc. After Skye, Islay is the largest island of the Inner Hebrides.

The islands are seeing a renaissance in their tourism, with the development of multi-million pound schemes on two new Golf courses and hotels, both on Islay at Machrie Hotel, adjacent to the airport and at Jura House, the ancient home of the Campbells, on Jura. In addition, a ninth distillery and visitor centre is now being built on Islay. All will add to the respective island economy, bringing jobs and more tourists.

Getting There

Calmac run services from Kennacraig on Kintyre to Port Ellen and Port Askaig on Islay (no direct service to Jura). Reaching Kennacraig involves a choice. Both alternatives involve two ferries. The more direct route goes via Arran with ferries from Ardrossan to Brodick and then from Lochranza to Claonaig on Kintyre, six miles or so from Kennacraig.

Kichiaran Bay, Islay

The alternative route involves taking the ferry across the Clyde from Gourock (west of Greenock) to Dunoon and then crossing Argyll, chiefly on minor roads through lovely scenery and then through the Kyle of Bute. There are memorable views including across to Bute itself before reaching Portavadie on Loch Fyne, the ferry to Tarbert and the last miles to Kennacraig. It is much longer, takes more time but the views may well be considered worth it. Don't overlook that the return journey may connect better with the Claonaig – Lochranza and Brodick ferries if you use the ferry at Port Ellen.

Islay and Jura are unspoilt islands, where the pace of life is slower; where the way of life seems more secure and quieter. There are none of the sleek modern petrol forecourts, no streets of modern multi-storey buildings, no glaring advertising hoardings. In other words, there are few trappings of modern consumerism. There is of course, good food to be had, the freshest of fish, the best of beef, lamb and venison. It also has the widest selection of whisky obtainable at a country inn anywhere, with the Ballygrant Inn offering a choice of c. 650 different malts.

Islay and Jura offer clean beaches, litter-free streets and fresh air as standard. It's quiet, but not living in the past. It attracts numerous cyclists and walkers, exploring some large areas of both islands where the lack of roads exclude cars. The low-lying island of Islay has a lot to offer walkers, cyclists, birdwatchers and much more for those wishing to explore. Then of course there are the whisky distilleries, offering tours and some with cafes as an additional facility.

For an island break, incorporating the opportunity to view various islands and Kintyre from the sea, why not visit Arran en route with the chance to stay overnight or longer there. The three ferries en route are part of the adventure of getting to Islay and Jura but with even a single ferry if travelling from Oban. These options includes calling at Colonsay, which may be of additional interest.

Islay also acts as a contrast to its close neighbour, Jura. The Paps of Jura are three very large hills visible from several miles away. Jura's population is small and mostly confined to the south east coastline. Much of the island consists of a belt of moorland stretching from north to the south. There isn't even a tarmaced road to the west coastline. You can walk there, use a mountain bike or go by boat, but abide by any rules of access for your own safety.

For much of the time, the ferry between the two islands criss-crosses the narrow section of the Sound of Islay all day long from Port Askaig on Islay to Feolin on Jura. There is also a passenger ferry from Tayvallich on the mainland to Craighouse on Jura during the summer months.

Kennacraig is simply a jetty constructed where there is sheltered water deep enough to take the boats against the coast of Kintyre. Conveniently, this happened to be virtually opposite the road from Claonaig. Currently, other than the administration office, there are few buildings here. If you are coming from Ardrossan on the mainland, upon landing on Arran, you need to travel north and take the short ferry from Lochranza to Claonaig. From here you cross Kintyre to reach Kennacraig. This latter journey is only c. 5 – 6 miles in length.

From Kennacraig, as the ship leaves for open water, the shoreline consists of a mixture of woodland, some pasture land and elsewhere, areas of rock outcrop. As the ferry pulls away, there is a mountainous backdrop to the north. The loch soon widens with Gigha island on your port (left) side. The ferry bears to starboard (right) as it heads for the Sound of Islay. If it is fine, the three Paps of Jura may be seen rising on your right. The ship is heading for the narrow passage of the Sound of Islay, likely to be indistinguishable ahead. Port Askaig is a small community. Its jetty serves ferries from Kennacraig, Oban, Colonsay and Jura. As the ferry sails up the Sound from Kennacraig, Islay is on the left side, Jura on the right. Sailings to Port Ellen do not head for the Sound of Islay, they head further to the south side of the island.

Getting There

By Sea

See the text above.

Calmac; ☎ 0800 066 5000 (www.calmac.co.uk).

Travelling to Scotland's west coast islands by Calmac ferry was voted one of the best public transport journeys in the world by Guardian Travel.

By Air

Flybe operate services from Glasgow airport: ☎ 0871 700 0535 (www.flybee.com).

Loch Ardnahoe

Islay Airport is situated at Glenegedale, close to Laggan Bay, PA42 7AS. ☎ 01496 30236. The terminal is open from 8.30 am to 6.00 pm (Mon – Fri), 10.00 am on Saturday and on Sunday from 4.00 – 6.00 pm. Bike hire at the airport is available.

In order to make all the connections, depending upon your choice of timings, you may find it necessary to spend a night on Arran, an opportunity you may consider one not to be missed. The alternative route involves going via the ferry from Gourock (west of Greenock) to Dunoon and then the narrow road to Portavadie with its ferry to Tarbert and the last few miles to Kennacraig. The climate is generally mild, but like all of this Scottish coast, subject to Atlantic gales. Islay is a quiet place, with clean, unspoilt beaches and a scenic coastline. It is somewhat hard to imagine that such a relatively small and unassuming place could have such an international reputation for its best known product, malt whisky.

Both Islay and Jura have now branched out into gin production: Bruichladdich distillery on Islay is producing The Botanist gin, distilled from 22 Islay botanicals. On Jura, Lussa gin is being produced from 15 Jura botanicals. Both islands have reacted relatively early to the renaissance of gin as a fashionable drink. Yet this has made no impact on the island in a physical sense. Islay and Jura remain beautiful islands. In addition to providing employment, the distilleries have a demand for grain and malt. The maltings in Port Ellen supply malt and local fields grow barley. Much of Islay is more low-level than Jura, but the latter makes up for this with its three Paps, reaching heights of 2,405ft/733m, 2,484ft/757m and 2,575ft/785m.

Islay is popular with walkers and cyclists. There is a good bus service and the roads are not heavily used. Close to Port Ellen is a 3 miles/5km tarmaced pathway from the town to Ardbeg, passing Laphroaig and Lagavulin distilleries on the way. It is popular with both walkers and cyclists and is fenced off from the adjacent road. If discerning walkers and cyclists know and use these islands, it is remarkable that, despite being so close to Glasgow, they seemingly remain untouched by commercialism, whisky production excepting. Nonetheless, modern if small, aircraft fly into Islay airport daily and the island is Wi-Fi served.

Most of the larger Scottish west coast islands retain evidence of prehistoric settlements. Despite its relatively small size, Islay has one of the finest surviving crosses in Europe. It is to be found by the side of the roofless Kildalton Church, a little under 5 miles/8 km beyond Ardbeg distillery.

Having reached the latter, stay on the road until a signpost alerts you that it is just on your right. The cross is definitely well worth going to see, its wheel-shaped upper section is the best surviving example in Britain to be complete. There is only another complete example and that is on Iona.

It is perhaps remarkable that Islay has the world's oldest Scotch Maturation Warehouse, dating from 1779. It also has one of the more recent distilleries dating from 2004. The ability to source all its requirements for production from the island must be a huge advantage.

Islay Distillery Directory

If you are travelling independently, it pays to book ahead and be clear which tour you wish to be on. For instance, you might like to be on a tour adjoining lunchtime at a distillery, which has a café. You can book local accommodation through the Tourist Visitor Centre. Some distilleries offer their own accommodation. Remember that accommodation, car hire and space on ferries are finite in number.

The Ballygrant Inn, situated near to Port Askaig in the community of Ballygrant is famed for having c. 650 different bottles of whisky to drink or buy. It includes a collection of various bottles of the former Port Ellen Distillery malt. The latter produced whisky from c. 1825 – 1929 and from 1967 – 1983. The inn offers accommodation and won the whisky Bar of the Year, 2015 Scottish Bar and Pub Awards.

The distillery briefing notes below are subject to change without notice but allow comparison of one site with another. On the south coast, three distilleries, i.e. Laphroaig, Lagavulin and Ardbeg, are situated close together. Caol Ila and Bunnahabhain are close together too, near Port Askaig, but the other three are more widely sited, two facing each other across Loch Indaal, i.e. Bruichladdich and Bowmore, with the latest distillery, Kilchoman, being situated to the north west of Bruichladdich. For details of the forthcoming Ardnahoe Distillery, see page 13

Laphroaig Distillery

Laphroaig, Islay, PA42 7DU

☎ 01496 302418

E: tourbooking@laphroaig.com

W: www.laphroaig.com

Established in 1815. Claims to produces the No. 1 Islay Single Malt. Situated on the B8016 just east of Port Ellen

Has a lounge, gift shop and museum

Café: No

Tours: Daily, March – Dec. 9.45 am – 5.00 pm; Jan – Feb, Mon – Fri. 9.45 am – 4.30 pm. Check Laphroaig.com for opening times during festive periods

Lagavulin Distillery

Port Ellen, Islay, PA42 7DZ

☎ 01496 302749

E: Lagavulin.distillery@diageo.com

W: www.discovering-distilleries. com/lagavulin

Established in the early 19th century

Shop: large range of Lagavulin merchandise and Lagavulin whiskies

Café: No

For tour times and opening hours: see website. March, April and October: Mon – Sun. – 9.00 am– 5.00 pm; May – Sept.: 9.00 am – 6.00 pm; Sat – Sun 9.00 am – 5.00 pm

Ardbeg Distillery

Port Ellen, Islay, PA42 7EA

☎ 01496 302244

E: see form on www.ardbeg.com

W: www.ardbeg.com

Established 1815

Shop and Visitor Centre as well as tours

Café: Yes, 10.00 am – 4.30 pm; last orders 3.45 pm. As distillery opening times

Opening times: Jan – Easter weekend,

This still lives out it's retirement at the entrance to Ardbeg

Nov – Dec: Mon – Fri:

Easter weekend – Oct – daily, 9.30 am – 5.00 pm. Site closed two weeks over Christmas

Accommodation: Seaview Cottage, once the manager's cottage within the distillery. Three ensuite rooms

Bowmore Distillery

School Street, Bowmore, Islay, PA43 7JS

☎ 01496 810441

E: wbd.bowmoredistillery@beamsuntary.com

W: www.bowmore.com

Shop: Yes, for Bowmore products

Café: Situated at side of street by distillery entrance

Tours: 5 tours on Mon – Sat, 2 tours on Sun. Tasting Session 1.30 pm during April – Sept.; Oct – March: 2 tours Mon – Fri; 1 on Sat. (open for bookings only in Jan – Feb), tasting session, Mon – Fri. 1.30pm

Accommodation also available: www.bowmore.com/visit at the Harbour Inn and Restaurant, which has seven bedrooms, and at a selection of cottages

Bunnahabhain Distillery

Port Askaig, Islay, PA46 7RP

☎ 01496 840646

E: see form on bunnahhabhain. com/contactus

W: www.bunnahabain.com

Shop: ☎ 01496 840557, open Mon – Fri 10.00 am – 4.45 pm. Reduced hours Nov – March

Café: No

Tours: April – Oct. daily; also tastings without tour, daily; Nov – March; also daily but reduced times

Standard, Dram and Tasting tours; plus Manager's tours which must be pre-booked

Founded in 1882. Situated by the sea; signposted off A846 just over 1 km from Port Askaig. Contact the distillery for visits

Caol Ila Distillery

Port Askaig, Islay, PA46 7Rl

☎ 01496 302769

E: Caolila.distillery:diageo.com

W: www.discovering-distilleries.com/caolila

Visitor Centre/Shop: wide selection of Caol Ila merchandise. Current range of whiskies available from the Visitor Centre. Established 1846

Café: No

Tour times and opening hours: see website. Open March – Oct: Mon – Fri 9.00 am – 5.00 pm; Nov – Feb: Tues – Sat 10.00 am – 4.00 pm

Situated on the Sound of Islay. Islay's largest distillery. Signposted off the A846 just out of Port Askaig

Distillery tours and tastings available throughout the year but pre-booking recommended

Bruichladdich Distillery

Islay, PA49 7UN

☎ 01496 850190

E: mary.mcgregor@bruichladdich.com

W: www.bruichladdich.com/distillery-tours-visits

Shop: Open all year round, but seasonal hours for shop; tours and warehouse experience Shop closed August and May. Also closed Sundays

Café: No

Semi derelict until 2001 but much of the old machinery from 1881 was still in place and brought back into use.

Whisky: Unpeated: Bruichladdich; heavily peated: Port Charlotte and Octomore

Gin: The Botanist Dry Gin. Made from 22 foraged island botanicals and 9 classic gin botanicals.

Call the Visitor Centre for one hour tour bookings

Situated on A847 coast road about 2 miles north of Port Charlotte

Kilchoman Distillery

Rockside Farm, Bruichladdich, Islay, PA49 7UT

☎ 01496 850011

E: Shop & tours: tours@kilchoman distillery.com

W: www.kilchomandistillery.com

Shop: Gifts, crafts and Islay tweeds

Café: Open all day

Kilchoman offer distillery tours plus a premium tour open 9.45 am – 5.00 pm, March – 30th Oct; open Mon – Fri, Nov – March

The first distillery built on Islay in 120 years. Its first whisky was made in 2005. This is currently the only distillery to complete all parts of the whisky making production on site. It even grows its own barley and highlights which fields are growing barley for the distillery

Situation: From Bridgend, take Port Charlotte road, A847 for just over 4 miles and then turn right onto the B8018. After approximately 2 miles the B-road branches right. Carry straight on for another 2 miles or so, passing Loch Gorm below on the right hand side, with the distillery being on the left. Above the lake after the B-road turns to the right, look left to see the small cliffs marking the northern end of The Rhinns of Islay, the upland of the peninsula, which stretches to Port Wemyss.

Ardnahoe Distillery
This will be a new distillery situated on a superb site overlooking the Sound of Islay, about half way between Caol Ila and Bunnahabhain. Planning permission was granted in 2016.

Bowmore to Port Ellen and the South Coast
This area includes two of the main centres of population (Port Charlotte being the third). It also includes the airport and one of the most important prehistoric sites in the country – the Kildalton Cross, the latter c. 800 years old. By comparison, the airport brings Islay to just over half an hour away from Glasgow. At the moment half of the island's distilleries lie in this area, together with another prominent landmark, the beaches of Laggan Bay which extend to five miles or so including the area where the airport is situated.

Ardilistry Bay, between Ardbeg and Kildalton Cross

Bowmore's Round Church.
There are only two of them in the
country, this and in Cambridge.

The rear of the Round Church
(*below*).

Laggan Bay, looking north from Kintra, south of the airport

The Oa bears the evidence of de-population, like some other parts of Islay

Bowmore is a small community with a main street, which rises up to a dominant landmark, its church, which is round. There is only one other round church in the country – at Cambridge. It dates from 1767 and holds various artefacts of the Rev. Donald Caskie, the Tartan Pimpernel, who through the Scots Kirk (Scottish Church) in Paris, helped at least 500 people escape from Vichy France during World War 2.

Bowmore has the island's hospital, a hotel, filling station and pharmacy and is the administration centre. It is a planned village of which the round church was a part. It is the home of Bowmore Distillery of 1779, although one wonders if its products were sustaining residents as far back as 1767/8 when the planned village was built.

The first couple of miles to Port Ellen from Bowmore curves around to the River Laggan. From the bridge there, the road, much of it the A846, runs in a straight line for some 7¼ miles/nearly 12 km. It was apparently planned as a railway, which was never completed. Much of the area to the north of the the B8016 road, which runs almost parallel to the north

Frederick Crescent, Port Ellen

of the A846 Port Ellen road, is over 1,000 ft/305m. in height, rising to 1,609 ft/491m. at Beinn Bheigeir. Much of it is uncultivated. Although it is incised by many streams, it lacks public roads similar to much of the land on Jura.

The Oa Peninsula (pronounced O) in contrast has a road which runs westward from the maltings at Port Ellen to a car park just short (a mile or so) of the far end. Here is a monument in memory of the men lost in 1918 when an American troopship, the U.S.S. Tuscania was torpedoed, as well as a Royal Navy troopship, the H.M.S. Otranto. Both were formerly luxury liners, the former being Scottish built in 1914 and torpedoed on 5th February 1918. She was carrying 384 crew and 2,013 U.S. Army personnel; approximately 210 men were lost. Many men were saved, as she took a life saving four hours to go down, 8 miles/13.5km north of Rathin Island, off Northern Ireland.

The monument also marks the loss of H.M.S. Otranto, a former passenger liner requisitioned by the Admiralty in August 1914. She was rammed in a violent storm by another naval troopship, the H.M.S. Kashmir, and her wreckage was forced ashore on 5th October 1918. Some 468 servicemen and crew were lost including 316 American servicemen. Bodies were piled by the storm up to 15ft/4.6m high on the shoreline. H.M.S. Otranto came ashore on the west coast of the Rhinns at Machir Bay.

Close to Port Ellen, the A 846 turns sharp left. To reach the sands of Laggan Bay, continue straight on to the t-junction. Turn right and then after a mile or so, right again. After a little more than 2 miles, turn left to Kintra and a Scottish Natural Heritage site. There is limited parking here and access through the dunes onto the sandy beach.

The maltings, from where the road across the Oa commences, dominates the approach to Port Ellen. It used to be a distillery on two separate occasions but now makes the Malt for all the island's distilleries. The malt is made from barley. It is allowed to germinate to the point when the starch in the barley has changed to what is called malt sugar. The latter, after drying, is then ground before moving to the next part of the production process, handled by the distilleries. The maltings are produced according to the specification provided by each distillery. The pagoda tops of two of the kilns still survive but are best seen from the road at the rear of the factory.

Upon passing the maltings, you can either follow the main road through the town, leaving along Lennox Street or go into the town to the harbour. At the top of Lennox Street is a school on the right and next to this is the beginning of the tarmaced path which leads to the three distilleries of Laphroaig, Lagavulin and Ardbeg. Otherwise proceed onto the harbour where the road leads around and passed the 19th century, crescent shaped cottages (including the Spar supermarket) in Frederick Crescent. Part of the feature of this area is the grassed area between the roadway and the shoreline. It adds to the area's attractiveness and one's memory of it. Port Ellen has a petrol/diesel station.

The distillery path passes by the three distilleries, reaching Ardbeg, the third distillery. There is a café open to the public. At Ardbeg the road becomes narrower. It runs along the coastline in places and after 4 miles /6km or so reaches Kildalton Chapel and its cross. It is signposted to the right and to a small carpark. The chapel is now roofless but has burial remains, some with stone carvings. The most important stone carving however is outside the chapel, the Kildalton Cross. This tall, free-standing stone, with its disc head (a circle of stone at the top) and its wealth of carvings is unique. It is one of the finest surviving crosses in Europe. They are also known as ring-headed crosses. It is thought that St. John's Cross in the churchyard of Iona Abbey may have been carved by the same school of sculptors, centred on Iona. The Islay cross is worth studying. An interpretation board enables you to do this.

If you have come this far by car, you can either return from here or continue a couple of miles or so to where the road runs out at Claggain Bay.

Bridgend to Port Askaig and the North

Having left the Bowmore area, at least descriptively, Bridgend is where the road divides for Port Askaig and the Rhinn Peninsula. The latter is lapped by the waters of Loch Indaal, Loch Guinart and to the west, the Atlantic Ocean. Bridgend has an hotel and filling station while the road to Port Askaig, the A846, has much of interest.

The Islay House Garden is run by the community and grows many vegetables and other plants for sale. The Ileach (the local newspaper) reports on which garden vegetables are for sale. You can also see the Ribbonwood tree, one of only two growing in the country. The garden is

open all the year round and free to visit. You can contact the garden on
☎ 07767 688051 or by Facebook (Islay House Community Garden). Also
at Islay House is The Square, where outhouses to the main house now
house a variety of businesses. These include Islay Ales, Elizabeth Sykes
Batiks, who also serve teas and coffees; Mackinnon's marmalade shop; a
gift shop and launderette; a carpentry workshop and more besides. The
Square is on the left, travelling towards Port Askaig and well signposted.

Further down the road to Port Askaig is the Islay Woollen Mill, situated
about a mile from Bridgend. Turn right where indicated and follow
the lane over the river to reach the carpark. The mill dates from 1883,
although a mill preceded the current one. It has some of the oldest textile
machinery still in production dating back to 1903. You can watch the
weaving process and select tweeds from over 100 different designs in
stock.

Watching the very old machinery weaving the cloth is very satisfying
especially when you can purchase the same design before you leave.
Unfortunately, although the mill has two vintage spinning jennys, they

Islay Woollen Mill

Port Askaig

Loch Gorm

Jura from Bunnahabhain Distillery

Saligo Bay

The Jura ferry at Port Askaig

are no longer run, but it is nice to buy items of clothing from a mill which still has such ancient machinery. A little nearer Port Askaig is Ballygrant Inn and its collection of different whiskies. Look out for it on your left.

From Ballygrant, the Glen Road cuts through the hills to reach the B8016, the Bowmore – Port Ellen road, south of Bowmore.

Beyond Ballygrant, a small community centred around the A846, there are three turns to the left of the road. The first gives access to an important site run by the Finlaggan Trust and the other two are signposted to two separate distilleries. The first is c. 0.75 mile beyond the Ballygrant Inn where you turn left and shortly afterwards turn left again to reach the site. The cottage has been rebuilt to create a visitor centre. A path and bridge give access to the castle and chapel (both ruined) of the Lord of the Isles. From here, the Lord (head of the Clan MacDonald) ruled the Western Isles and much of the western coast of Scotland in the Middle Ages.

The second signposted lane is c. 3 miles/5km long to Bunnahabhain Distillery with memorable views to the hills of Jura. The road ends at the distillery. The final road, just prior to Port Askaig, is to Caol Ila distillery, the largest on the island, and to Persabus Pottery.

Ballygrant Inn

Port Askaig consists of the ferry building, including toilets plus post office and general store including newsagents. It also has the Port Askaig Hotel, which claims to be the oldest licensed premises on Islay. Its garden stretches down to the water where you can enjoy food and/or drink, in the warmth of a sunny day enjoying memorable views across the Sound of Islay. The tranquility is periodically interrupted by the Jura ferry creating an interesting distraction as it goes about its business, whilst the CalMac Ferry does the same thing but on a much larger scale and far fewer number of times.

The Rhinns of Islay

Despite the south being able to count on three distilleries and the fine sand of Laggan Bay, the Rhinns of Islay has its own fine bays, a distillery and the benefit of a circular road to the tip and back. Moreover, Portnahaven has one of the islands finest views, to the Orsay island lighthouse plus a resident quantity of curious seals that pop up and down out of the harbour water with regular precision.

The Rhinns provide a backbone of higher land whilst the circular road runs down the eastern side heading for Port Charlotte. It hugs the coast for but little of its length south of Port Charlotte and is well inland on the western side. Nonetheless, it allows you to appreciate the landscape as you travel along.

The upland nature of The Rhinns ends just south of the road, which leads to Kilchoman Distillery. North of here is the largest of inland lochs on Islay – Loch Gorm which is freshwater, together with Loch Guinart which is a sea loch. At the southern end of the latter is a tiny community called Craigens, where Islay Oysters have a shop and a self-catering cottage. There are roads on each side of Loch Guinart which allows good opportunities to view the birdlife. Islay Oysters is on the beginning of the eastern side.

Loch Gorm is the island's largest inland lake and is fished for brown trout. Just past the loch the road reaches the distillery. It is possible to visit here and it also has a large and busy café which extends beyond the shop. This distillery uses home grown produce and started production in 2005.

Continuing past the distillery, the road continues on towards Machir Bay. The next turning to the left ends at Kilchoman Church with its c. 700 year old cross. The church was last used in 1977 and is now roofless. South-west of here will be seen the cross in the Military Cemetery. Here lie 74 graves of which 71 are from the H.M.S. Otranto which went down in Machir Bay (see also p. 17). The more ornate gravestone marks the burial place of Captain E. G. Davidson, the ship's captain. The American soldiers initially buried here were subsequently repatriated or now lie in the U.S. Military Cemetery at Brookwood, Surrey. (Wikipedia: Kilchoman Military Cemetery)

The majority of the population of The Rhinns peninsula in the north west of Islay are to be found in Port Charlotte and Portnahaven where the number of fishing boats in the harbour gives one a good idea of the maritime nature of the local economy. At Port Charlotte, at least to the north of there, the Bruichladdich Distillery looks across Loch Indaal towards the equally white painted Bowmore Distillery. Both produce a spirit revered internationally and with a devoted following, as elsewhere on Islay and equally on Jura. Port Charlotte also has a well appointed youth hostel, also in a former distillery and a restaurant.

Elsewhere on The Rhinns, a pastoral economy is prevalent to the visitor. The road system allows the opportunity of a better exploration. At Portnahaven, the road runs along the north-western side, although not along the coast, having reached there on the opposite eastern side. This eventually turns to run back to Port Charlotte. This has its convenience but prevents reaching Machir Bay by road from the south.

Leaving Bridgend the road, the A847, skirts around the head of Loch Indaal. A look to the right would seem to show abandoned cliffs and the former head of the loch. Soon the A8018 is passed and a mile and half or so beyond the large white painted distillery of Bruichladdich is reached. Approximately two miles further on is Port Charlotte, with the Museum of Islay Life one of the first buildings reached on the right and up steps and looking out to sea. There is carparking on the left of the road. The community is elongated with pastel painted terraced cottages lining the road.

Portnahaven is about seven miles further on with views from the road over the cliffs to the sea. At the latter, the alignment of terraced houses situated above the harbour and with the large lighthouse seeming built at the end of the houses (it is an optical illusion, it is built on the island of Orsay), sets a scene ready for many photographers. Another scene waiting for most cameras is the colony of seals in the harbour. Their curiosity is a most endearing sight. The lighthouse was built in 1825 and is 29m high and can be seen from 24 miles away (Wikipedia: Lighthouses of Islay) The terraced houses are later and many photographers owe a debt of gratitude to a builder with an eye for symmetry. The village has a small craft shop and a pub serving food.

Port Charlotte

Port Charlotte lighthouse (Rubh' an Duin lighthouse)

Museum of Islay Life

Portnahaven

Portnahaven

A minor road leaves Portnahaven for the small community of Kilchiaran about a mile south of Machir Bay, which is reached by a footpath from here. The road then runs about four miles across the peninsula to reach Port Charlotte. The bottom of the peninsula particularly the area south of Port Charlotte is dotted with small hillocks. The O.S. map is equally dotted with the word Cnoc. Perhaps this is hardly surprising as Cnoc is the Gaelic word for a small hill. Approximately four miles north of Portnahaven, where the road on the western side of the peninsula rises uphill having crossed the River Lossit, the terrain is rather interesting and there are several cnoc features to your right.

JURA

Jura is one of the larger islands of the Inner Hebrides yet one of the least populated, with c. 260 inhabitants (1901: 560.) Its most noted physical feature is the Paps of Jura. The highest is Beinn An Oir (2,575ft/785m), meaning mountain of gold. The other two are Beinn Sheunta (hallowed mountain) and Beinn a Chaolois (mountain of the sound).

The south coast near the ferry at Feolin

The Jura Hotel

Lagg

Jura is only cultivated on a coastal strip running from the south of the island around to the south-east. Virtually all the rest is peat-covered moorland heath and rock. It has its use however. The stalking of deer is now a very lucrative source of income. The wild expanse of moorland has historically been divided into six estates, with one estate now having been divided. There are c. 5,000 deer and the annual cull is c. 1,000 animals (red deer, both stags and hinds). Provision for tourism on Jura is largely confined to stalking and fishing (by rod).

As one author put it, '…*there is little on Jura for unarmed car-bound tourists to do …'*. There is however one hotel in Craighouse and pub (in the Jura Hotel). This small community also has a licensed shop and the distillery (for tours and purchases). So unless you are walking or wild camping (and confining yourself to requirements from the estate owner) book early at the Jura Hotel or take advice from Bowmore Visitors Information Office (or as advised by that office in winter months).

The East Coast

Jura Church

Most visitors go for a few hours and used to take in Jura House Gardens before going on to Craighouse. However it is closed. Jura House is being restored and a top class 18-hole golf course is being constructed. The road becomes a track at Ardlussa, continuing to Barnhill where George Orwell wrote '1984', which was published in 1949. When landing at Feolin, look out for the standing stone nearby.

The Gulf of Corryvrekan

This is a whirlpool situated off the north coast of Jura between the latter and the island of Scarba. It is the third largest whirlpool in the world. Although a visitor attraction, maritime traffic needs to use caution when making passage through the Sound.

At certain times of the year, there is a noticeable imbalance in the level of the sea either side of the islands. This creates a strong tidal stream. This may also be associated with a lot of noise which is sometimes rather loud. The tidal stream may be dangerous, creating the whirlpool. The 'West Coast of Scotland Pilot' states *'When the tidal streams jet through the gulf, navigation at times is very dangerous and no vessel should then attempt this passage without local knowledge. The passage through, from west to east is not so risky as that in the opposite direction.'*

Above: The Distillery

Inset: Craighouse

Below: Tarbert Bay

Published by
Guidelines Books & Sales
11 Belmont Road, Ipstones, Stoke on Trent ST10 2JN

☎ 07971 990649 email: author.porter@gmail.com

ISBN 978-1-84306-564 7

British Library Cataloguing in Publication Data: a catalogue record for this book is available from the British Library.

Printed by Hobbs the Printers Ltd, Totton, Hants

The author acknowledges the assistance and photography of
Helen Maurice Jones in the production of this guide.

The bay at Laphroaig